Flashlight On Drama & Film
A Drama for Situation Analysis Guide

Ekpe Inyang

Langaa Research & Publishing CIG
Mankon, Bamenda

Publisher
Langaa RPCIG
Langaa Research & Publishing Common Initiative Group
P.O. Box 902 Mankon
Bamenda
North West Region
Cameroon
Langaagrp@gmail.com
www.langaa-rpcig.net

Distributed in and outside N. America by African Books Collective
orders@africanbookscollective.com
www.africanbookscollective.com

ISBN: 9956-792-81-0

© Ekpe Inyang 2015

Table of Contents

Table of Contents

Preface

Every human being or, generally speaking, every living creature is an actor or actress at one level or another on the stage of life and time. As acting is an activity common to all life forms and a distinguishing feature of drama, it goes without saying that the definition of drama as "an imitation of real life" is apt and unchallengeable.

Any moment in our lives we find ourselves caught in the performance of one type of drama or another. In fact, every human activity has a dramatic undertone, and it is only by being keen observers of what goes on naturally around us can we become successful actors/actresses or dramatists in a modern and professional sense.

Drama is flexible and applicable to a wide range of contexts. As an environmental educationist working for conservation projects, I used drama as a tool for sensitisation and mobilisation of local communities and the general public to take positive steps towards environmental conservation.

The use of drama in this respect simply means affording the target audiences opportunities to analyse environmental situations, presented through drama, with a view to enabling them to make informed decisions and take responsible actions in similar situations in the real world. This constitutes the guiding principle of Drama for Situation Analysis (DRASA), with *Flashlight on Drama and Film* as its training guide.

Ekpe Inyang, 2004

Introduction

DRASA is an initiative developed by the author as inspiration from a consultancy assignment, in 2003, by from the German Technical AID Agency (GTZ, now GIZ). The first attempt was to make a rapid evaluation of the Korup Project and present the results in the form of drama in order to make the information available to a wider target audience. It has been noted that often projects are evaluated but the final reports end up in shelves that are not accessible to a cross section of the stakeholders, especially the rural beneficiary communities. By giving each stakeholder a chance to contribute to the evaluation process and later the opportunity to analyse the overall situation as presented in a more easily accessible and interpretable form, DRASA underscores the importance of participatory project assessment (PPA) in an effort to bring about the desired change in any given organisational set up.

DRASA does not claim to have developed a new set of methods for this initiative. It simply exploits what has long been employed by experts of Theatre for Integrated Rural Development (THIRD), and applies this to an area that might not have seen the bold footprints of drama before. The initiative starts with a simple form of research to obtain materials for the development of a play script (the creative process) and proceeds through training of players to enable them to gain an understanding of the play as well as arm themselves with tools for acting (the interpretative process) to presentations of drama to target audiences (the reproductive process). Figure 1 gives an illustration of these processes. The effort may stop at the level of drama presentations or proceed to the shooting of a film, depending on the financial resources, and / or the objectives of the initiative.

The creative process

The reproductive process

The interpretative process

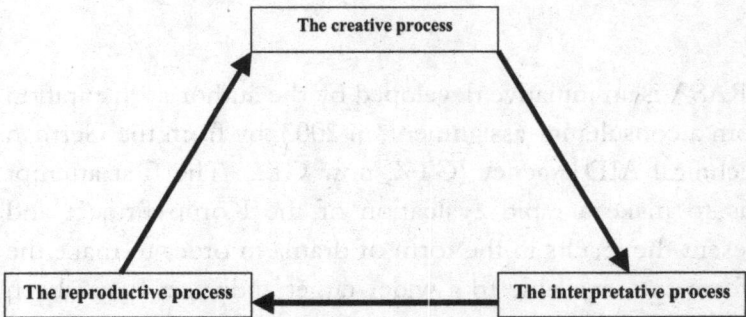

Figure 1: Processes in drama production

The development of *Flashlight on Drama and Film* was inspired by the response of both the drama trainees (who are now proud film players!) and the general public regarding the performance of *The Last Hope*, a play depicting the life of the Korup Project, on stage and as a film production.

Flashlight on Drama and Film succinctly describes the journey in the drama effort. It is divided into three parts. Part One looks at the development of the play script from the research stage. Part Two describes the stages involved in interpreting a play, including the skills, techniques and terminology of acting, from a simple definition of drama. Part Three gives a rundown of the stages in rehearsing and presenting a play, either as stage drama or film production.

Part I

The Creative Process

The development of a play script is the first stage in DRASA. Its starts with a simple research effort to obtain materials relevant for the drama piece. Like any form of research, the first step is to establish the main objective of the investigation. Figure 2 describes the creative process.

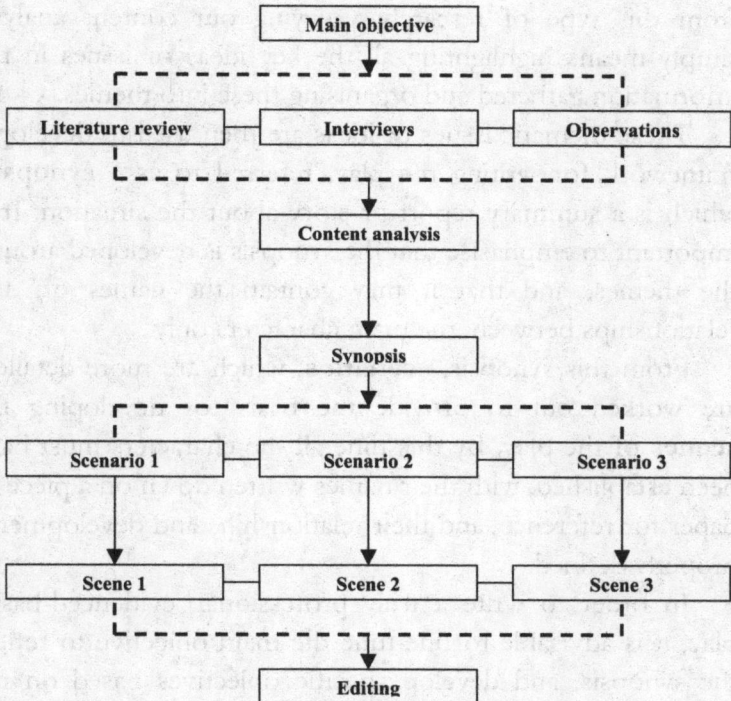

```
                    ┌─────────────────┐
                    │  Main objective │
                    └─────────────────┘
                             │
    ┌────────────────────────┼────────────────────────┐
┌──────────────┐    ┌─────────────────┐    ┌──────────────┐
│ Literature   │────│   Interviews    │────│ Observations │
│ review       │    │                 │    │              │
└──────────────┘    └─────────────────┘    └──────────────┘
                             │
                    ┌─────────────────┐
                    │ Content analysis│
                    └─────────────────┘
                             │
                    ┌─────────────────┐
                    │    Synopsis     │
                    └─────────────────┘
                             │
    ┌────────────────────────┼────────────────────────┐
┌──────────────┐    ┌─────────────────┐    ┌──────────────┐
│ Scenario 1   │────│   Scenario 2    │────│ Scenario 3   │
└──────────────┘    └─────────────────┘    └──────────────┘
        │                    │                    │
┌──────────────┐    ┌─────────────────┐    ┌──────────────┐
│   Scene 1    │────│    Scene 2      │────│   Scene 3    │
└──────────────┘    └─────────────────┘    └──────────────┘
                             │
                    ┌─────────────────┐
                    │    Editing      │
                    └─────────────────┘
```

Figure 2: Stages in the creative process

A **literature review** on the area of focus and site could be the next necessary step. This serves as an entry point and helps bring clarity and direction to the area under investigation. This could then be followed by **interviews**, **observations** or other appropriate research approaches, in order to gather more in-depth and up-to-date information relating to the pressing and underlying issues.

Next is to analyse the data. **Content analysis,** as described by Gillham (2000), followed by narrative/descriptive techniques, is an appropriate analysis tool for the type of information that is normally gathered from this type of research. Carrying out content analysis simply means highlighting all the key ideas or issues in the information gathered and organising these into themes.

These thematic issues or ideas are then used to develop a framework for writing the play, referred to as a **synopsis**, which is a summary report or story about the situation. It is important to emphasise that the synopsis is developed around the themes, and that it may contain the names of, and relationships between, the main characters only.

From this synopsis, **scenarios**, which are more detailed, are worked out to provide the basis for developing the **scenes** of the play. By this time all the characters must have been established, with their names written down on a piece of paper for reference, and their relationships and developments properly defined.

In order to write a truly professional, evidenced-based play, it is advisable to fine-tune the main objective to reflect the synopsis, and develop specific objectives based on the scenarios. A professional, evidence-based play is that which is written based on a premise or hypothesis developed from the main objective.

After having established what are set out to be achieved, both in general and specific terms, the whole business of play writing could easily find its appropriate course, depending on the level of motivation and inspiration of the author. A lot of the work is done mentally, crafted and refined over and over again, before putting the ideas on paper or any other devise.

At the ripe moment, the dialogues and dramatic actions develop naturally to fit each character. It is expedient not to force things out; they should be ready to come out, naturally. A creative person is like a labouring woman in a maternity ward, who should be prepared and patient enough to labour and wait until it is the right time for the baby to be born.

Once a lot of thinking has been done, with respect to the objective (s) of a given scene and the characters and their interactions in various dramatic situations, putting down the thoughts becomes as easy as taking down the minutes of a meeting.

Editing may start at any time. Some authors prefer editing a scene once it has been developed; others prefer drafting all the scenes before doing the editing. From my experience, this might simply not be a matter of choice. Ideally, editing after all the scenes have been written is preferable, but sometimes ideas cease flowing and it might be necessary to stop at such moments and browse through some finished parts, for relaxation or so to speak. Such refreshing interludes have the advantage that they might help one gain some insights into how best to proceed with the rest of the work.

It is important to stress that sufficient time should be allocated for editing because, to achieve good finishing, this should include editing for: a) grammar and mechanical accuracy, b) appropriateness and clarity of dialogue, c) characterisation, d) dramatic structure, e) dramatic techniques, and f) play length.

Part II

Section 1: Getting started

To be able to attempt an interpretation of a play script, it is necessary to understand first of all in what genre it falls, and what the underpinning philosophy and definition of the genre is. Figure 3 shows the stages involved in the interpretative process.

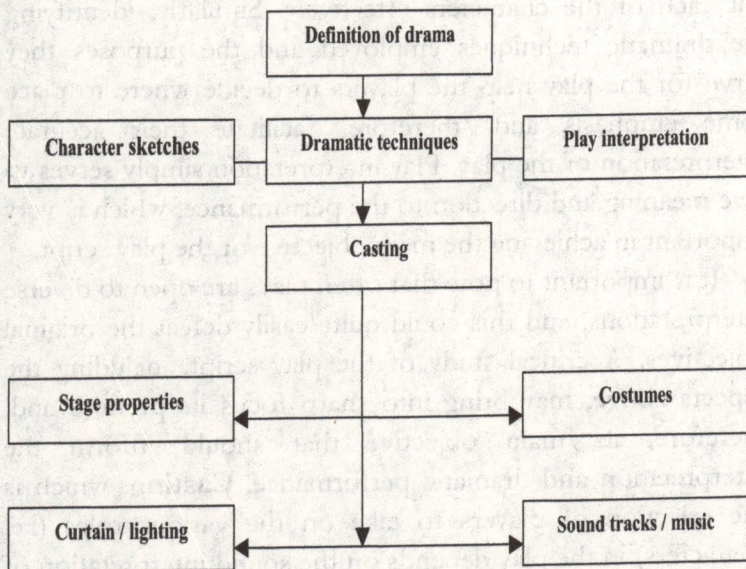

```
                    ┌─────────────────────┐
                    │  Definition of drama │
                    └──────────┬──────────┘
                               │
┌──────────────────┐  ┌────────▼──────────┐  ┌────────────────────┐
│ Character sketches│──│ Dramatic techniques│──│ Play interpretation │
└──────────────────┘  └────────┬──────────┘  └────────────────────┘
                               │
                    ┌──────────▼──────────┐
                    │       Casting        │
                    └──────────┬──────────┘
                               │
┌──────────────────┐          │          ┌────────────────────┐
│ Stage properties │◄─────────┼─────────►│      Costumes       │
└──────────────────┘          │          └────────────────────┘
                               │
┌──────────────────┐          ▼          ┌────────────────────┐
│ Curtain / lighting│◄─────────────────►│ Sound tracks / music│
└──────────────────┘                     └────────────────────┘
```

Figure 3: Stages in the interpretative process

can be said with confidence that the script produced ... under the broad genre drama, which is simply defined as **an imitation of real life**. It should also be established that only some aspects of the real life situations can be presented in a dramatic form, and that these must often undergo some creative surgery (but without serious factual injury) in order to appeal to the audience.

Then comes a dissection of the play script. This begins with **character sketches**, and continues to identification of **dramatic techniques**, and an attempt at **play interpretation**. To do a character sketch simply means to assign adjectives to each character (e.g. proud, pompous, etc.). This provides the basis for motivating the players to act out each of the characters effectively. Similarly, identifying the dramatic techniques employed and the purposes they serve for the play help the players to decide where to place some emphasis and, therefore, facilitate their accurate interpretation of the play. Play interpretation simply serves to give meaning and direction to the performance, which is very important in achieving the main objective of the play script.

It is important to note that often plays are open to diverse interpretations, and this could quite easily defeat the original objectives. A critical study of the play script, including the aspects above, may bring into sharp focus its premise and, therefore, its main objective that should inform the interpretation and dramatic performance. **Casting**, which is the selection of players to take on the various roles (i.e. characters) in the play depends on the sound interpretation of it. A cast should be chosen for the benefit of the audience rather than as a way of rewarding or bribing the players (Nelms, 1958).

Once a cast has been chosen, the players should be asked to identify the **stage properties** or **props** (e.g. a walking stick) and **costumes** (e.g. a loin cloth) they need to use scene after scene. This should be followed by sketches of the scenes, which are pictorial depictions of the directional development of the scenes. All this affords the players an opportunity of developing an even deeper understanding of the play, which potentially increases their performance of the roles they have to play to move the drama forward.

At this juncture, decisions should also be made about either to use a **curtain** or **lighting** to divide scenes, with some training given on the techniques of handling these. It should be noted that lighting could be used also to achieve effects such as depicting the time of day during which an event is taking place (e.g. evening). Similarly, there should be a selection of **sound tracks** and **music** to be used to achieve certain effects that, combined with the lighting effects, help to define the atmosphere of the play.

Section 2: The game of acting

A new football player cannot start the game of football and be sure to do it well without having an intimate understanding of the playground. By the same token, a drama player cannot be effective without a clear understanding of the stage geography (Figure 4).

Upstage Right	Upstage Centre	Upstage Left
Downstage Right	Downstage Centre	Downstage Left

Figure 4: Stage geography
Source: Nelms (1958)

This is very important because it informs the selection of positions for the players. Positions serve to add more emphasis or importance to some characters and events over others.

After mastering the stage geography, there are some terms, skills and techniques that need to be understood. These are presented step by step in Figure 5.

```
                    ┌─────────────────┐
                    │ Stage Geography │
                    └─────────────────┘
                             │
                             ▼
┌───────────────┐   ┌─────────────────┐   ┌───────────────┐
│  Movements    │───│  Stage business │───│   Groupings   │
└───────────────┘   └─────────────────┘   └───────────────┘
                             │
                             ▼
┌───────────────┐   ┌─────────────────┐   ┌───────────────┐
│  Blocking in  │───│     Covering    │───│  Distraction  │
└───────────────┘   └─────────────────┘   └───────────────┘

┌──────────────────┐                      ┌───────────────┐
│ Voice management │──────────────────────│    Timing     │
└──────────────────┘                      └───────────────┘
┌──────────────────┐                      ┌───────────────┐
│ Voice projection │──────────────────────│     Cues      │
└──────────────────┘                      └───────────────┘
                             │
                             ▼
                    ┌─────────────────┐
                    │ Synchronisation │
                    └─────────────────┘
```

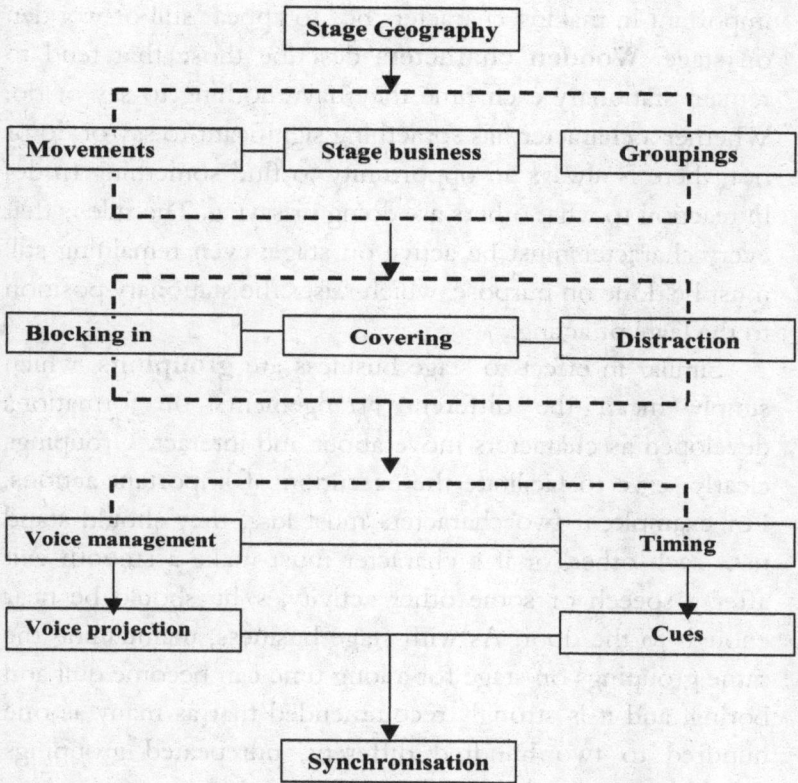

Figure 5: Tools for acting

Stage geography directs **movements** on stage, which
range from characters making entrances and exits to walking
or running to meet other characters. Movements, therefore,
involve taking different positions on stage as against **stage
business** that may be executed without any significant
change in position. Stage business, which includes nodding or
shaking the head, winking the eye, or making such other
gestures as a form of response, reaction or signal, is very

9

important in making characters not to appear still or wooden on stage. **Wooden characters** describe those that tend to remain stationary each time they have nothing to say or do. Whether a character has something significant to say or do or not, there is always an opportunity to find something to do, in reaction to what others are doing or saying. The rule is that every character must be active on stage; even remaining still must be done on purpose, which raises the stationary position to the level of acting.

Similar in effect to stage business are **groupings**, which simply mean the different arrangements or formations developed as characters move about and interact. Groupings clearly serve to facilitate the execution of important actions. For example, if two characters must kiss, they should stand near each other, or if a character must make a smooth exit after a speech or some other activity, s/he should be near enough to the door. As with stage business, maintaining the same groupings on stage for a long time can become dull and boring, and it is strongly recommended that as many as one hundred to two hundred different, unrepeated groupings should be executed in a full length play to add to its colour and grandeur.

In executing groupings, enough attention should be paid to **blocking in**, which simply means getting the characters arranged in positions where they can easily be seen by the audience. Effective blocking in also means that the audience sees not only the characters but also what they are actually doing, no matter how insignificant these might appear to be. These may be as trivial as the wink of an eye, but insofar as they form part of the force that drives the play, it requires that characters take positions where these actions do not go unnoticed. Otherwise there would be missing links in the flow of action.

The opposite of blocking in is **covering**, which describes a situation where a character (including his or her important stage business) is completely or partially hidden behind another, from the perspective of the audience. This can be dangerous as important aspects of the play could be missed out. Another thing that may cause this to happen is **distraction**. Distraction is when an unimportant but attractive action is performed concurrently with an important one, during which time attention is naturally drawn away from the action that is supposed to be highlighted at that point in time. For example, one character may be signalling to another to indicate it is time for them to leave, while yet another character is at the same time (by way of improvising a stage business) wiping his or her nostrils with a handkerchief. Naturally, the "wiping of nostrils" could direct attention away from the "signal to leave". And when the two characters finally leave it might be difficult to know why, due to the missing link. However, covering, and to some extent distraction, could also be used as a technique to disguise a faked action, such as a knife-thrust of a murderer (Nelms, 1958).

Other important aspects in the interpretative process of drama are **voice management** and **timing**. To achieve a high level of managing their voices, some players may need ample training while others may not need training at all. The first purpose of voice training is to ensure that a person sitting in the back of the auditorium is able to get what a player upstage is saying. In this case, there is need to practice **voice projection**, which simply means increasing the force of the voice in order to be heard from a distance. Voice

11

management may also be geared towards imitating some particular characters, such as an authoritative person or a drunkard.

Similar in importance to voice management is **synchronisation**. This means that when a character says something that requires an accompanying action, this should be done in such a way that there is harmony between the speech and the action. In other words, the speech must synchronise with the action. Put in yet another way, speech and action should go on simultaneously, and in a smooth and natural way.

The final consideration is timing. This means doing the right thing at the right time; that is neither doing it too early nor too late. This brings in another element—**pause**. A pause is a moment of silence (which may be as important as speech), the length of which is determined by a number of **beats**. For instance, we may consider one beat as a **short pause** and three beats as a **long pause**. Effective timing depends as much on the proper execution of (including acting on) these beats as they are on **cues**. A cue is something a character sets at each situation to remind himself or herself when to start doing something. Commonly, the end of a speech by one character provides a cue for the next character to speak or act. Other cues may simply be sounds or some forms of action.

12

Part III

The Reproductive Process

After having mastered the basic elements of acting, it is now time to start rehearsals of the play. The stages in the reproductive process are shown in Figure 6 below.

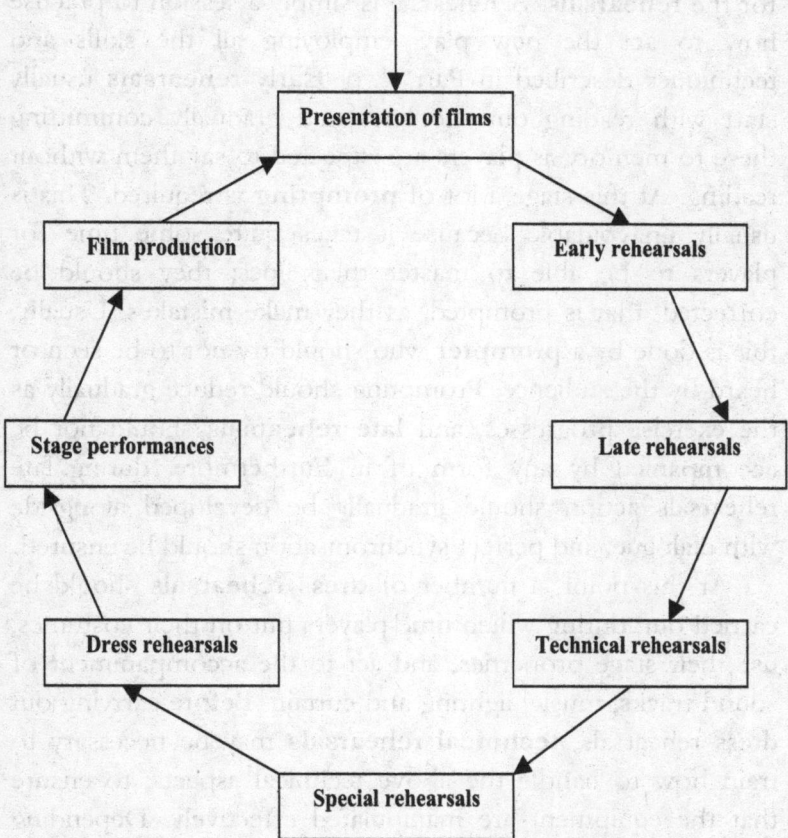

Figure 6: Stages in the reproductive process

This could start off with **presentation of films** to stimulate and motivate the players. These shows also serve to reinforce some of the skills the players might have developed already. To achieve this reinforcement, the attention of the players should be drawn to the performance elements that arise at every important moment in a film.

During the films presentation, every effort should be made to help the players build up confidence to prepare them for the **rehearsals**. A rehearsal is simply a session to practise how to act the new play, employing all the skills and techniques described in Part Two. **Early rehearsals** usually start with reading out the lines and gradually committing these to memory as players are expected to say them without reading. At this stage a lot of **prompting** is required. This is usually unavoidable because it takes quite some time for players to be able to master their lines; they should be corrected, that is prompted, as they make mistakes. Usually, this is done by a **prompter** who should try not to be seen or heard by the audience. Prompting should reduce gradually as the exercise progresses, and **late rehearsals** should not be accompanied by any form of it. Furthermore, during late rehearsals action should gradually be developed alongside with dialogue, and perfect synchronisation should be ensured.

At this point, a number of **dress rehearsals** should be carried out, during which time players put on their costumes, use their stage properties, and act to the accompaniment of sound tracks, music, lighting and curtain. Before carrying out dress rehearsals, **technical rehearsals** may be necessary to train how to handle the above technical aspects, to ensure that the equipment are manipulated effectively. Depending on the play, it may be necessary also to conduct **special rehearsals**, especially where there are scenes that require training in, say, fighting or dancing or movements by large crowds. Special rehearsals are also necessary where the effort has to proceed to the shooting of a film **on location**, that is in the natural setting. Some practice is needed to learn how to use the natural space, and to do so effectively.

Film shooting appears to be easier for the players than is **stage performance**, but perhaps far more energy demanding and possibly boring. Easier because, the players do not need to achieve a mastery of their lines before this can be done. Energy demanding and boring because a single action can be shot several times, from different angles, to select the best during editing. It is advisable always to start a speech again, in a different angle, from the very beginning, and for the cameraman to start recording again one count before the player starts acting...as a rule! This leaves overlaps on tape, which are easy to cut off during editing, rather than leaving out sections as a result of both the cameraman and the player starting on the same count. Sections left out during shooting cannot be reintroduced, unless there are repeat shots of those particular segments. Missed out segments may only be identified during editing, which is often done miles away from the shooting site. Imagine what it means to correct the mistake, especially in financial terms!

In shooting a film, there is often emphasis on close-up (**CU**) to ensure that facial expressions and other aspects that need to be shown are focused. For instance, if someone stresses that s/he is married, it would be useful to focus briefly on the wedding ring or some other sign to confirm this, if it is the truth. This suggests that a film emphasises, and indeed includes, more details than a stage performance, and is definitely nearer to real life. There are aspects that are not possible on stage but which form an important and interesting part of a film. For example, how can you realistically show people drowning in a river on stage? There are so many of such examples where only report back techniques are employed in stage presentations, whereas they are conveniently and effectively presented in films.

Some scenes require that shooting is internal (**INT**); that is, done in enclosed areas such as buildings or vehicles. This may require good lighting, and the limited space in the enclosure might be a constraint on time and effort. The only advantage is that internal shooting can take place even in poor weather. Scenes involving external shooting (**EXT**), that are done in open spaces free of any form of enclosures, such as roads or motor parks, may not require lighting, not if there is sufficient sunlight. The only constraint is that poor weather, especially that which is wet, works against the effort. Generally, it saves time and money to carry out film shooting during periods of good weather.

The different angles, such as wide angle (**WA**), and close-up (**CU**) add colour and variety to the film, but take a lot of time both during shooting and in the course of editing. And, in the final analysis, the time taken to shoot and edit a film may be much, much longer than that which is used to carry out several rehearsals and present as many as ten or more stage performances!

Another important difference between the two forms of presentations is that with film the audience is not immediately known and so the efficacy of the effort cannot be easily and immediately assessed. But, on the other hand, with a stage performance the audience and the players are present together, albeit with seemingly no interaction between the two groups, but a rough assessment of the efficacy of the performance can easily be made either by direct observation of responses from the audience or through some form of question and answer session at the end of the performance.

This is a form of **monitoring and evaluation**, which is an important but often neglected aspect of most of such interventions. It is important to take this seriously by going back to the target audiences after a number of months to find out what is happening within the communities, what people are now doing differently, as a result of their exposure to the drama performances or film presentations.

Conclusion

Drama is increasingly becoming a popular intervention in many human endeavours, due largely to its applicability to a wide range of contexts—sensitisation and awareness, situation analysis, community development, conflict resolution, and so on.

DRASA is dedicated to the evaluation of projects and presentation of the results in the form of drama so as to reach out to a wider target audience, which includes all the stakeholders. The underlying philosophy of DRASA is based on the assumption that by presenting the overall project results in a form that is accessible and interpretable by all the stakeholders, particularly the beneficiary communities, there is a possibility that they would eventually be mobilised to take collective actions as a result of the common experience they will have gained through the drama.

Despite their differences in objectives and emphases, DRASA and THIRD share similar methodology, philosophy and general principles. DRASA is mainly concerned with presenting the evaluation results of a project in drama form and in ways that might ultimately bring about some change in society, including that which is necessary for the development of a new form of organisational structure and behaviour.

Bibliography

Bentley, E. (1983) The life of the drama. New York: Atheneum.

Boulton, M. 1960. The anatomy of drama. London: Routledge and Kegan Paul.

Burns, E. (1972) Theatricality: a study of convention in the theatre and social life. London: Longman.

Davis, R. 2001. Developing characters for script writing. London: A & C Black (Publishers) Limited.

Eyoh, N. (1984) Hammocks to Bridges: An experience in theatre for development. Bets & Co (pub) Ltd. Yaounde.

Finnegan, R. (1992) Oral traditions and the verbal arts: A guide to research practices. London: Routledge.

Gillham, B. (2000) Case study research methods. London: Continuum.

Gooch, S. (2001) Writing a play. London: A & C Black (Publishers) Limited.

Inyang, E. (2000) Drama for the sensitization and mobilization of local communities for conservation: Lessons from the Banyang-Mbo Wildlife Sanctuary Project. A report prepared for the Wildlife Conservation Society.

——— (2002) Community drama as instrument for community sensitisation and mobilisation. Submitted for inclusion in Jua R. M. (Ed.). Emerging perspectives on Cameroon drama and theatre: 1950—present.

——— (2003) Lessons learnt in the establishment and implementation of a community-based conservation model for the Banyang-Mbo Wildlife Sanctuary in southwest Cameroon. A consultancy report prepared for the Wildlife Conservation Society.

———— (2003) The life of the Korup Project (1986—2003): A dramatic presentation. A drama/film consultancy report prepared for the GTZ.

———— (2005) The Game. An unpublished film script.

Inyang, E. and Eni Etim (2005) The Game . In Ekpe Inyang The game and water na Life. Limbe: The Cure Publishers.

McGuire, B. (2000) Drama: Student handbook. Cambridge: Pearson Publishing.

Nelms, H. (1958) Play production: A handbook for the backstage *worker: A guide for the student of drama*. New York: Harper & Row Publishers, Inc.

Vansina, J. (1961) Oral tradition: A study in historical methodology. Chicago: Aldine Publishing company.

Appendices

Take a close look at the following excerpts of *The Game,* as a play script and *The Game* as a film script. What differences can you find between them?

Appendix 1: *The Game* as a play script

Scene One

In front of the Chief's palace. Councillors and other villagers are having a meeting with CONSERVATION EDUCATION OFFICER and two SENIOR WILDLIFE OFFICERS. The SENIOR WILDLIFE OFFICERS are dressed in green uniforms, with their ranks conspicuously displayed. Loud argument from CROWD.

CHIEF *(Authoritatively)*: Please, let us get the full story from the Officers.

Silence.

CONSERVATION EDUCATION OFFICER: Thank you, Chief. *(A pause)* As I was saying, the whole idea of bush meat trade is not good. *(A short pause)* It is even against the law. Your village is

known all over for its big bush meat market.

(Looking round) I know it's hard to convince anyone here that the animals will one day finish. Most people argue that

23

hunting has been going on here from generation to generation, and the animals are still plentiful. But *(Emphatically)* do you think that today the animals are still as plentiful in your forest as they were, say, ten years ago?

DRUNKARD *(In a drunken tone):* Officer *(Laughing mockingly), some done already go for country for* die people.

Appendix 2: *The Game* as film script

EXT. VILLAGE — DAY.

We float through a village street flanked by a mix of thatched and zinc houses and finally focus on a thatched one from which PA EWON emerges, carrying a stool in hand and staggering slightly. Just in front of the house, he trips, staggers violently and leans on the wall, letting the stool fly in the opposite direction.

CU: PA EWON's face clearly confirms his drunkenness. We move down his body and view his trembling legs as he leans on the wall. Gradually, he manages to stand up erect, obviously angry about what has happened to him.

PA EWON
(Standing, arms akimbo)
What am I really going to gain from there? How many glass them go give me sef?
(CU: Looking at the stool)
Do you think I will leave you behind?

CU: PA EWON *picks up the stool and starts staggering away.*

We follow him until he disappears gradually at a bend.

EXT: CHIEF'S PALACE — DAY.

CHIEF, Councillors and other villagers are having a meeting with CONSERVATION EDUCATION OFFICER and two WILDLIFE OFFICERS. The WILDLIFE OFFICERS are dressed in green uniforms, with their ranks conspicuously displayed. There is a loud argument from MEN.

CHIEF
(Authoritatively)
Please, let us get the full story from the Officers.

WA: MEN in silence, with a mix of approving and disapproving communications going on only in gestures.

CONSERVATION EDUCATION OFFICER
Thank you, Chief.
(A pause)
As I was saying, the whole idea of bush meat trade is not good.
CU: CHIEF. His anger-laden face.

CU: CONSERVATION EDUCATION OFFICER, as he is taking a deep breath.
It is even against the law. Your village is known all over for its big bush meat market.

WA: MEN. Their spontaneous reactions are unanimously negative.

25

CU: PA EWON: We pick him as he has just arrived. He places his stool next to the officers.

WA: MEN in a burst of laughter.

PA EWON
(In a drunken tone)
So it is you people again, eh? I hear you go about seizing and auctioning people's meat.

CHIEF
Will you shut up, Pa Ewon! If you won't behave yourself this time, you will be forced to leave.

CU: PA EWON as he curls his body on the stool in obvious submission, whispering to himself at the same time.

PA EWON
Let me shut my mouth before someone heaps another fine on my head.

CHIEF
Go ahead, Officer. We are here to listen to you.

CONSERVATION EDUCATION OFFICER
Thank you, Chief. I know it's hard to convince most people here that the animals will one day finish.

MBURU
But why must they finish?

26

CONSERVATION EDUCATION OFFICE
That doesn't surprise me.

CHIEF
But look, Officer, hunting has been going on in this land from generation to generation, and we still have lots and lots of animals.

WA: MEN in corroborative shouts.

PA EWON
(Looking round at MEN)
What are these people supporting?
(A pause)
Papa Chief, that one no be true. Officer, some important beef them done already de enjoy country for die people.